PRAISE FOR
GIULIANI

"A lively new biography explores how the man once celebrated as 'America's mayor' fell into disgrace."

—Louis Menand, *The New Yorker*

"[Kirtzman] possesses the salient advantage of having covered Giuliani close up for decades, witnessing his evolution from an Eliot Ness crimebuster to the Sheriff of Rottingham. . . . What this biography conveys is that Rudy's breaking bad wasn't a sudden turn to the dark side. The hairline cracks in his moral and behavioural make-up were there from the outset."

—James Wolcott, *The London Review of Books*

"Cuts through the myth and caricature that has too often defined Giuliani . . . As a former television reporter for NY1, Kirtzman knows the man better than the pundits who have often scratched their heads about the Giuliani they thought they knew."

—Chris Megerian, *Los Angeles Times*

"Masterful and engrossing . . . capture[s] what made the man tick and what led to his fall from grace. Kirtzman's critique is leavened with bittersweet impressions and references to Giuliani's accomplishments."

—Lloyd Green, *The Guardian*

"Kirtzman's Giuliani is a tragic figure, one whose lack of fear spelled doom as he aged. . . . What happened to Rudy Giuliani? The more pressing question posed by Kirtzman's book is what happened to us, that it took so long to see it."

—Devlin Barrett, *The Washington Post*

"The book is loaded with psychological and farcical detail. . . . It's an unsparing portrait, but it isn't an attack. Tying everything together is Kirtzman's assessment of what has propelled both the successes and failures in his subject's saga."

—Chris Smith, *Vanity Fair*

"The same 'fanatical sense of righteousness' that propelled Rudy Giuliani's rise set him on the road to ruin, according to this richly detailed biography. . . . A comprehensive and alarming portrait of Giuliani's downfall."

—*Publishers Weekly*

"With a cinematic made-for-TV sense of scene and pacing, gossipy insider revelations, and sharp analysis, Kirtzman vibrantly depicts the sad and tawdry unraveling of Giuliani's reputation."

—*Booklist* (starred review)

"A veteran political reporter ventures an answer to the question so many have asked in recent years about Rudy Giuliani: 'What happened?' . . . A sad tale, expertly told, of corruption, bad judgment, avarice, and treason."

—*Kirkus Reviews* (starred review)